EXTREME WEATHER

# TORNADOES

NORWOOD HOUSE PRESS

JACK WILLIAMS

**Cataloging-in-Publication Data**

Names: Williams, Jack.
Title: Tornadoes / Jack WIlliams.
Description: Buffalo, NY : Norwood House Press, 2026. | Series: Extreme weather | Includes glossary and index.
Identifiers: ISBN 9781978576865 (pbk.) | ISBN 9781978576872 (library bound) | ISBN 9781978576889 (ebook)
Subjects: LCSH: Tornadoes--Juvenile literature.
Classification: LCC QC955.2 W555 2026 | DDC 551.553--dc23

Published in 2026 by
**Norwood House Press**
2544 Clinton Street
Buffalo, NY 14224


Designer: Rhea Magaro
Editor: Kim Thompson

Photo credits: Cover, p1. ALBYPC, JP Midwest Storm Chaser /Shutterstock.com; p. 5 dangrasan9/Shutterstock.com; pp. 6, 10 Domenichini Giuliano/Shutterstock.com; p. 7 SingerGM/Shutterstock.com; p. 8 Dennis MacDonald/Shutterstock.com; p. 9 Joe Belanger/Shutterstock.com; p. 12 NickJulia/Shutterstock.com; p. 13 Silverszay/Shutterstock.com; p. 14 HarrisonJeffs/Shutterstock.com; p. 15 Bilanol/Shutterstock.com; p. 16 Joko P/Shutterstock.com; p. 18 lafoto/Shutterstock.com; p. 20 Photoguru73/Shutterstock.com



Printed in the United States of America



CPSIA compliance information: Batch #CWNHP26: For further information contact Norwood House Press at 1-800-237-9932.

# TABLE OF CONTENTS

## WATCH OUT!

There is a **thunderstorm**.

Spinning **wind** whips down from the clouds.

Watch out! It is a **tornado**.

# WHAT IS A TORNADO?

A tornado is one of the strongest **forces** in nature.

Its winds blow faster than the fastest sports car.

No one knows for sure how a tornado starts.

There may be two air **masses**.
They twist together. They **rotate**.

A tube of air forms. It gets bigger and faster. It makes a **funnel** cloud.

If funnel clouds drop to the ground, they become tornadoes.

# WHY ARE TORNADOES DANGEROUS?

Tornadoes happen all over the world. They happen all across America.

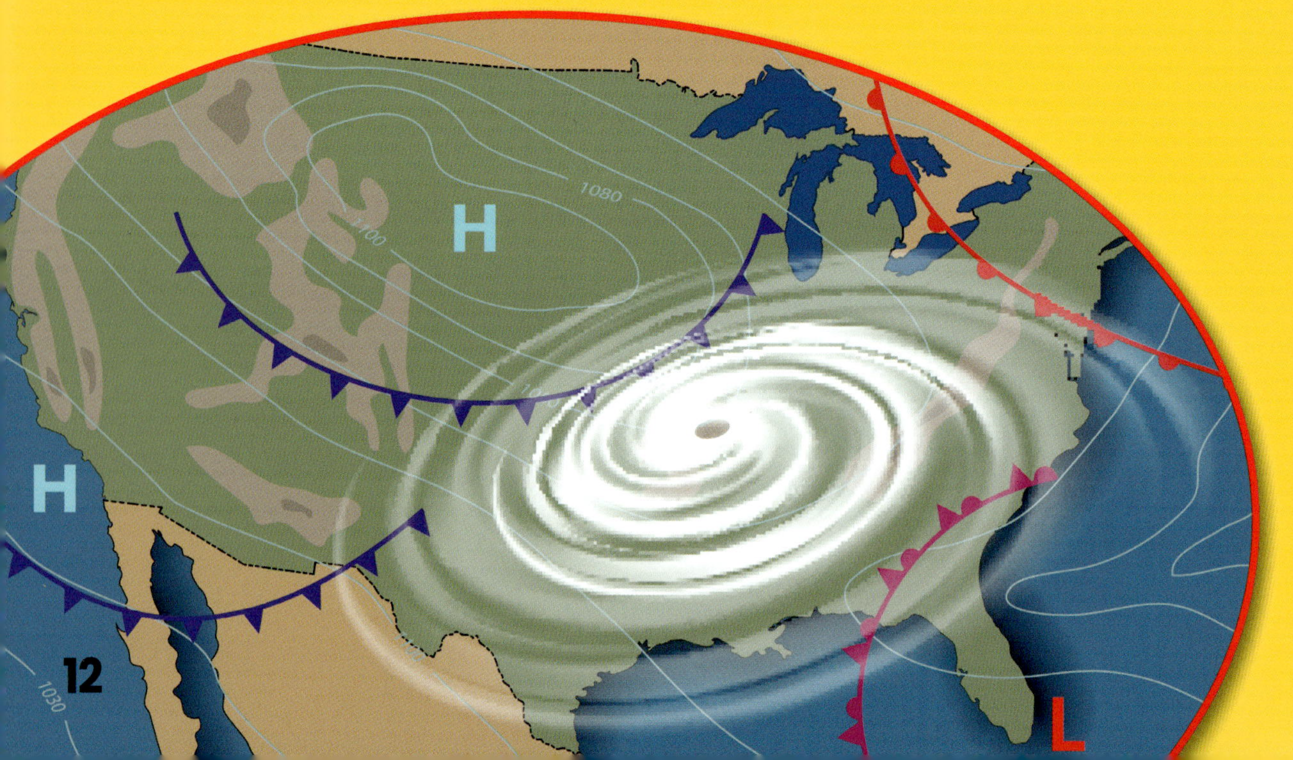

Tornadoes can lift anything in their path. They can **destroy** trees, cars, and buildings.

Tornadoes carry glass and other **debris**. It can fly out. It can hurt people and animals.

NEMESIS
HIMAWARI 8 EH 17/03/2022 07:00UTC
© Badan Meteorologi, Klimatologi, dan Geofisika - 2022
Temp(C)
110 E
120 E
140 E
Vektor Angin
Animasi Wilayah 1 |...Animasi Wilayah 2... | Animasi Wilayah 3 |...
Detail...
Animasi Wilayah 5 |...

## HOW TO STAY SAFE

Pay attention to the weather **forecast**.

A tornado watch means that a tornado could happen.

A tornado warning means a tornado is nearby.

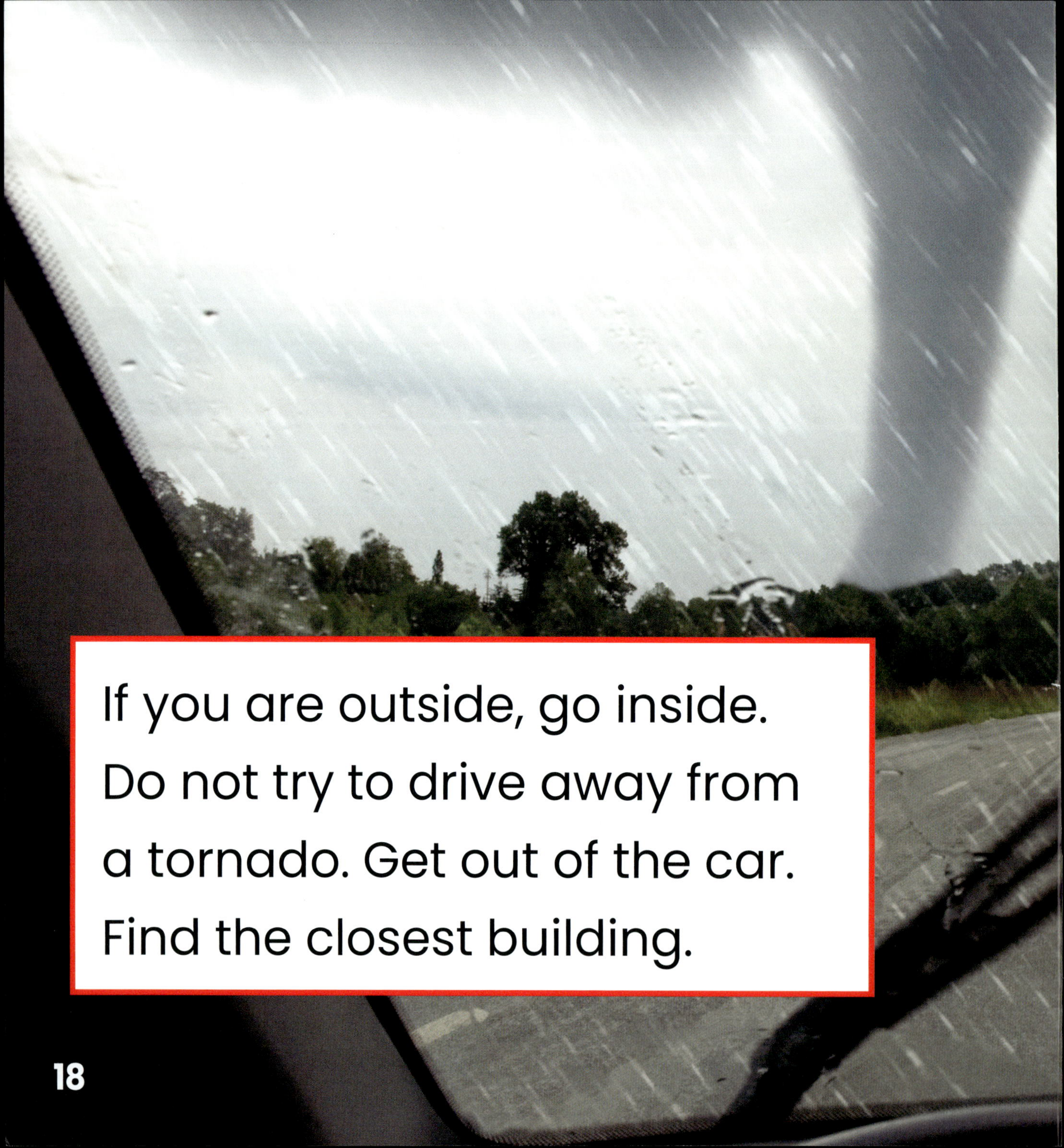

If you are outside, go inside. Do not try to drive away from a tornado. Get out of the car. Find the closest building.

Go to the basement if there is one. If not, go to the lowest floor.

Find a room with no windows. Cover your head.

Do not come out until the storm has passed.

# GLOSSARY

**debris** (duh-BREE): pieces of broken things like wood, glass, and metal that are left after something is damaged or destroyed

**destroy** (dih-STROY): to break something completely so it cannot be used anymore

**forces** (FOR-siz): strong powers that can push, pull, or move things

**forecast** (FOR-kast): a report that tells what the weather will be like in the future

**funnel** (FUHN-uhl): a shape like an ice cream cone, wide at the top and narrow at the bottom

**masses** (MA-siz): large amounts that move together as one big group

**rotate** (ROH-tate): to spin around and around like a top

**thunderstorm** (THUHN-dur-storm): a storm with loud thunder, bright lightning, and heavy rain

**tornado** (tor-NAY-doh): a destructive windstorm that appears as a dark cloud shaped like a funnel

**wind** (wind): moving air that you can feel when it blows

## THINKING QUESTIONS

1. What is a funnel cloud?
2. Where can tornadoes happen?
3. What can tornadoes destroy?
4. What is a tornado watch?
5. What should you do if you are outside during a tornado?

# INDEX



# ABOUT THE AUTHOR

Jack Williams is curious about all things in nature, especially the weather! He checks the weather forecast every day. He used to be a police officer, so he knows how important it is to watch out for danger and stay safe.